Both Sides of the Niger

Andrew Kaufman

SPUYTEN DUYVIL   *New York City*

ACKNOWLEDGMENTS

Some of these poems, often in earlier versions, appeared, or are scheduled to appear in the following journals:

Grey Sparrow: "Against Dying," "Both Sides of the Niger," "Cafe Baobab," "Children in the Forest," "Drumming," "On the Hut Walls in Togo."

Skidrow Penthouse: "Grease," "Sand," "The Shade of the Niger," "Thirst"

I owe profuse thanks to Thomas Lux and Tsipi Keller for reading and offering pitch-perfect suggestions on earlier versions of this manuscript. The book would not otherwise exist in its current form. I am much indebted to Stephanie Dickinson, Rob Cook, Chris Belden, and the other members of the Renegades writers group for their word-by-word-and-line-by-line suggestions and responses to most of these poems, often at their earliest, most challenging stages.

I am thankful to the National Endowment for the Arts, whose fellowship helped make it possible for me to spend the time I did in West Africa

Last but not least, I am deeply indebted to the many people in Benin and Togo, in particular, who made this book possible by welcoming me into their homes and sharing so much of their lives with me, and to numerous others I met in passing, whose kindness and patience were often not just welcoming but revelatory. I am especially indebted to the villagers of Nadoba, Togo, and to those of Peperkou, Benin, in particular the village chief and his family, and the to children in this village who trusted me to be their goalie.

Library of Congress Cataloging-in-Publication Data

Kaufman, Andrew.
 [Poems. Selections]
 Both sides of the Niger / Andrew Kaufman.
    pages cm
 Poems.
 ISBN 978-1-933132-50-1
 I. Title.
 PS3611.A824B68 2013
 811'.6—dc23
   2012043138

To the memory of my mother,
Dorothy Kaufman,
who set me on my way toward these poems
without knowing it.

CONTENTS

Foreword

Called the Dark Continent in the 19th century, Africa in the 21st century seems almost as inscrutable. Africa, short-hand for want and destitution, for disease and civil war. Yet how little we truly know and it is into this great unknowing that comes the shiveringly, brilliant poetical gift of *Both Sides of the Niger*. Mali, Benin, and Togo constitute its geographical epicenter. The poet Andrew Kaufman allows us to experience where he journeys by becoming the observing eye and ear. It is as if he has metamorphosed his corporeal self into camera and recordation device, transporting the reader to West Africa.

In a long shot we see the Niger River through the plane window illustrating Kaufman's sophisticated technique that allows us to witness in panorama what we will later see in varying distances. What strikes one beyond the exquisite use of language and unmistakable craftsmanship in "The Shade of the Niger" is the cinematic detail. "From the air/it is the vast body/ of a snake," that "loops motionless,/not a breath or twitch in the desert sand." Then in "On the Hut Walls in Togo" Kaufman curates and culls, moving in for close-up frames. A toy red tractor. Botticelli's Mary. Idi Amin. It is about seeing in the deepest way. Ears, eyes, brain, heart. At the same time, the poet establishes a constant forward motion, a dialogue between the visitor and the villagers visited.

No hotels or tour buses mediate the distance between the poet and desert dust, "the countryside, flat and treeless." Kaufman travels alone. He sleeps in huts and eats from the communal pot. Like the explorer Richard Francis Burton, the poet immerses himself in the everyday of the land and its inhabitants. He seeks out destinations with place names like

"The Mausoleum Outside Natitingou, Benin" or "The French Military Cemetery of Ouidah, Benin."

This is not the office landscape where we denizens of the overdeveloped world spend most our waking hours interacting with computers—little gods that mediate our experience of reality. In West Africa the elements bear witness to their own power, and what is essential dominates. A number of poems bear their names. "Thirst," "Sand," "Wind," and "Want." Guides point the way, sometimes offering up the relics of the colonial period that are seen like haunted obelisks. A spectral detritus.

> *Do you go*
> *for the old German cemetery*
> *in the bush? The big stone house*
> *in the forest, with columns? You look*
>
> *for the old jail*
> *in the woods.*

The poet often uses italics as counterpoint to indicate dialogue between the seer and seen. The italicized voice is sometimes that of a child-guide speaking with such simplicity that the affect is one of superlative beauty and excruciating vulnerability. This voice revealing volumes about what is miraculous and heartbreaking in the everyday world "where each day burns more than the last." This structure of guide and traveler works brilliantly throughout. Always there are gods, and while the West lives in a god-drained public square, here the poet tells us, "A god is needed." The child guide explains what the mud god requires. "He demanded the white feathers/of a baby bird/we stuck these/in his head."

The reader undergoes an inner and outer transmutation. While Kaufman makes no judgments, no naming of victims or villains, neither is there sanitizing. "You. Money. Money. You give me money." We are presented with the whole spectrum of sight, sound, sense and so unused are we to actual primal experience that it can jolt us awake. To feel these poems is perhaps to be disturbed. Yet the poet strives for a contrast between the poverty and beauty of everyday life. He tells us that "tatters of goat skin, and plastic bags sat in water's viscous stench." He contrasts this with men in "billowing white gowns, filled, like sails with sunlight." The primitive violence erupts in the "Open Sewers of Mopti" where a crowd chases a thief with rocks and knives. This poem is placed side by side with one of the collection's most life-affirming and delicate, "The Hello Song."

These are poems that make the reader shudder; they are seductive and hypnotic, mesmerizing and rhythmic. They are melodic, emotionally resonant, they are discordant. Their echoes linger long in the mind. They are singing poems. Kaufman has written one for the ages, if there are ages to come for humanity on our planet.

A stand of pink blossoms
turned to butterflies
as we approached.
A yellow butterfly
settled on the trail
and became a leaf.

Stephanie Dickinson
Co-Editor, *Skidrow Penthouse*

There are more things in heaven and earth, Horatio
than are dreampt of in your philosophy. But come ...

William Shakespeare

There are no foreign lands. It is only the traveler who is foreign.

Robert Louis Stevenson

I

AGAINST DYING

1.

Because of the gods and spirits
that surround Kudadze's home...
Because his family was curious,
since I am light skinned, and, by local standards, rich.
Or because Kudadze is kindly and patient,
or since I am a stranger, or because
his family expected money...

Because it was already noon
and I was leaving the next day,
he and two friends led me to his home
through miles of heat and dust.
When I could no longer ride his rusted bicycle
they walked with me.
When I could no longer walk in the sun
they sat with me in the shade. *Not much more,*
they smiled, *Not much more.*

2.

Because the countryside, flat and treeless,
had been surrounded by warlords
and slave-traders
since before they counted years—
the people still build their homes
as fortresses—dried mud walls
too high to be scaled, too thick
for arrows and muskets.
Since dry mud cannot protect
against what is not visible,

to keep out hostile spirits
they etched tightly bunched lines
across the walls.
Taking a double bond against fate,
they scarify the lines
across their foreheads and cheeks.

Because the spirits of sickness
seep like water
between etched lines,
A god is needed,
Kudadze labored to explain
in pidgin French.

A priest is needed
to know which god.
An augury is needed
to inform the priest
what food and drink
the god must have.

3.

Beside the doorway a sheaf of grain
assures the plentitude of rain.

Monkey skulls beside the sheaf
watch the home against the thief.

Crockery crumbling in a tomb
feeds the dead as in the womb.

4.

At first featureless and limbless,
the large mud god
they had formed rested
before the house. *He sees and hears,*
Kudadze tells me, *eats and breathes*
through the hole
that is his navel.

The priest said he demanded cowrie shells—
we set these into the mud
of his body.

He demanded wood
to form his legs—
we brought two trunks.

He demanded the white feathers
of a baby bird—
we stuck these
to his head.

He demanded water—
we set the kettle
before him.

He demanded millet—
we poured the porridge
over him.

He demanded goat's blood—
we spilled the blood
upon him.

He demanded meat—
the goat's skull
is beside him.

He demanded his children—
the small gods
are around him.

5.

Beneath my feet
I noticed the shallow breaths
of a week-old puppy,
rust-brown like the dirt and dust,
struggling to stand
and failing.

6.

A boar's skull beside the door
assures the hunt as before.

The gazelle's tracks in the shaman's sand
predict the bounty of the land

The shaman reads the face and sum
of what is passing and to come.

7.

Children and an old woman
surrounded me from a distance,
too shy to come closer.

I became aware of a friend or brother
of Kudadze approaching me,
then a soft, frightened chicken
pressed into my arms, and a voice
in a language I do not know,
repeating what could have been,
You, please, take, and *gift.*

BOTH SIDES OF THE NIGER

Trachoma, typhoid, bilharzia, more Latin names—
until age twelve, usually before three,
both sides of the river, they die just the same.

The village chief, hunched on his dirt floor, complained—
You give pencils but give no money.
Schistosomiasis, filariasis—more Latin names.

A boy who giggled at his laughter on my tape
and one who tried to drown a wild donkey—
both sides of the Niger the two died just the same.

Near a copse of cypress trees the wind changed
the voices in the leaves to a sea—
leishmaniasis, TB, cholera, still more Latin names...

They die in the pirogue, leave too late
to Mopti, the chief said. *No doctor. No money,*
Both sides. This river. Sick. Then dead. The same.

The bully who smirked, *Ka-boom! Bin Laden. Plane!*
A scared girl, her *"Duck, duck Goosie!"* always me.
Dengue fever, river blindness, malaria, non-Latin names—
both sides of the Niger they died just the same.

THE VOODOO MARKET OF LOME, TOGO

Since they of course know
that foreigners have no use
for blanched skulls of monkeys,
rats, and apes, coiled
snake skeletons, nor the furry heads
of dogs, arranged, row after row, by size...

and only a witch doctor can read the auguries
that tell if the spirit
needed to fight the spirit
of a curse or sickness
demands bone or blood
of what animal...

two young men blocked my way,
saying they ran the market,
demanding what came to two weeks of wages
for hard labor—
Then we show you.
Then we explain
the secrets.

There was nothing I could say, nothing
to negotiate or bargain.
They knew I had taken a moped taxi
fifteen kilometers to come here.
I took from my day pack the diabolo,
the small toy I kept with me
to amuse children and befriend their parents,
and spun it on its string
until it made the sound of a small fierce wind,

then hurled it high into the choking dust
and caught it on the string. *You,*
I said to both men, *You try this.*
And as they backed away,
I told them, *You cannot do this.*
You are frightened. Even to try.

It is nothing but a game, one replied.

No, No, it is magic! I cried out,
and forty vendors from stalls throughout the market appeared
and watched. *Not one person here can do this!*
With all your potions and spells, I taunted, *With all your voodoo,*
not one person! They watched in wonder
as I threw it higher and higher,
so that each time I caught it
I had to take a few steps
toward the market's center.

The moped driver came and whispered into my ear,
Look! From here you see everything,
and he gestured toward the jars of organs
and entrails, the open-jawed, sun-leached
skulls of crocodiles, and makeshift tables of *gris gris*
and talismans now beside us. In the awful
heat and glare of noon, I mistook
the impossibly huge vertebrae and femurs of an elephant
for a dusty construction site.

Everything, the moped driver whispered,
with the secret delight
of a person's one true friend. *Everything.*
Look more! From here you see everything.

CHILDREN IN THE FOREST

When I left the last village
voices of children
in the foliage
grew louder
than the white-water river.

Twenty found me
and crowded around—
Tell us your name, they sang out happily,
Do you go
for the old German cemetery
in the bush? The big stone house
in the forest, with columns? You look
for the old jail
in the woods?

Can you tell me, I asked,
Are there spirits in the bush?
On the tallest tree
there was not a single leaf,
just branches bearing a spiky green fruit
I had never seen.

A boy picked a beautifully colored beetle
from a stem and held it before me.

Yes, many, they answered.
Can you tell me their names?

I heard a buzzing in the ground foliage
like that of trapped bees
probing for an exit
to the sun.
A stand of pink blossoms
turned to butterflies
as we approached.
A yellow butterfly
settled on the trail
and became a leaf.

Alinka lives in the waterfall,
on the mountain, a boy replied.
He protects the village.

Agboth captures those wandering alone
in the forest. He beats them to death
and eats them. He comes at night
to the village.

A foot-long blossom,
containing a red tongue
opened like the moist mouth
of paradise.

At the brook on the road
lives the spirit of a white man
who died in a motorcycle accident,
but he is neither good nor bad.
He does nothing..

Boys pointed to broad, spreading leaves,
each with twelve fingers, and said,

This tree, too, has fruit
but it is poison.
A boy plucked a locust
from a leaf, held it before me
and said, *We prepare it like this,*
as he deftly tore off each leg and wing,
then tossed it to the ground,
laughing. The tombstones were broken,
weed-choked, effaced,
their metal plaques gone.
Trees glistened in the sun
Through what had been
the plantation house roof.

The wall of a sitting room
had been used as a blackboard
for first grade arithmetic.

A Western toilet,
hauled into the kitchen
contained the remains
of someone's recent vomit.
The large parlor room
was scattered with goat shit,
graffiti, and a few singed aluminum cans.

I heard a rush of insects
sounding like a distant wind.

The German prison
stood solid, impenetrable
in the foliage.

Atami causes sores and pox,
like these. Two boys rolled up their pants legs.
There are many, many smaller spirits.
But since the woods were burned
long ago, there are no gods
in here. Now there is God, only one God,
in the sky.

II

THIRST

We crossed stretches of river
that a river abandoned.
Bent against the current,
we followed a jagged channel
of wind. Far off was a sea

fed by torrents of sun
in which a man could drown.
*Where, Ahmed, are the ancient
grave sites you promised?*
What I had taken for dwellings
were dwellings of shadows

where the sand gives way
to sandy cliffs. *Come in under the shadow
of this red rock*, taunts a famous poem,
*and I will show you something different
from your shadow rising before you...*
But you can tell it's near noon
when there is no shadow.
Ahmed answered only, *To kill a gazelle
with no gun—find a tourist
with a four-wheel,
find the gazelle—
floor the gas—one hour,*

*two hours, when the gazelle cannot run
it falls down, then you kill it
with your knife. You get four wheel, my friend,
I show you.* What we approached
all morning was not a cluster of huts,

I now saw, as the shadows
that were their sloping roofs
vanished. *Where, Ahmed,*
are the thousand-year ruins
the guidebooks say nothing about?

You say 'Yes,' but whatever
you point at turns to sand.
I searched the distance
for where the sea
of desert divides
from the billowing sea of sky.

His eyes are brackish swamps.
His three small brothers
pass day after day
memorizing Koran
in Arabic they don't know—
half humming it in the shade
on the tedious way
to paradise. The road ahead
was not a road but a path
of boulders. The path ahead

was not a path but a scar
across slow, sandy breakers
of sun. *How long, Ahmed,*
how long and far
before the blue of the sea
is the sea?

The Shade of the Niger

From the air
        it is the vast body
                of a snake,

loops motionless,
        not a breath or twitch
                in the desert sand.

But from a pirogue
        the river
                is silt brown,

slow-moving
        through the dry season,
                but wide enough

for fishermen
        to call it
                the sea,

as in, *Do you have the sea*
        in your country?
                Where it bends

it is stagnant and clouded
        like a half-hearted scheme
                resolving slowly

into a puddle. Toward noon
        it is a heavy brown skirt
                covering a cluster of women

to the waist
        as they wash themselves
                and a few pots.

My pirogue moves among them,
        searching
                the mud

for a landing.
        Their nipples
                are chapped, coarsened,

cracked, chewed, and stretched.
        They snigger and cackle.
                Their breasts hang like paper bags.

They cannot ask
        for money—
                the hidden pockets

of the river
        will hold no banknotes.
                I stare

into the scarified
        eyes below their eyes,
                the white outlines

shaped like almonds,
        cut into both cheeks
                with a razor blade.

I try to guess their ages
      within ten years
            the way my grandmother

taught me
      to look at the teeth
            of shelter dogs.

The river's shade is deep enough
      for a person to pee in secret,
            those beside her

noticing nothing
      but the quick warmth
            of a little current.

Neither shy
      nor forward—
            like the river

in the desert
      they are neither welcoming
            nor hostile.

I squat with them
      at night
            in the dirt,

their fingers twisting
      the dorsal fins
            off a pile of fish

still quivering,
　　　　small enough
　　　　　　　　to be bait.

Moon and lantern light
　　　　catch in the white underbellies
　　　　　　　　and in the outlined

 second set of eyes.
　　　　The huts are the light brown
　　　　　　　　of the drying river bed,

made from its mud.
　　　　Night enclosed
　　　　　　　　by windowless adobe

is a crawl space
　　　　between river and river god.
　　　　　　　　Dawn starts as a slit in a thatched roof.

And the day,
　　　　like everyday,
　　　　　　　　is burning.

ON THE HUT WALLS IN TOGO

A series of animals
with their names in English:
Dog, Parrot, Goat, Cat, Camel.

*

A red-haired two-year-old
in a red baseball cap and matching pants
rides a toy red tractor
in front of a 1950s American
split level and its restful lawn.

*

Above the caption, *Look at the face*
and the hand of this man. They reveals his character,
stands a beneficent Osama bin-Laden,
with his beard and robes.

*

Botticelli's Mary
gazes from the heaven
of a magazine cut-out.

*

A collage of bodies with gaping wounds,
and troops aiming assault rifles at villagers
is captioned, *General Taylor's soldiers*
killing people.

*

In hut after hut, the de facto
president-for-life gazes severely
out of a campaign poster.

*

A buxom white girl
in a cowboy hat with feathers
and a fetching little denim jacket
as the sun explodes
on her bare midriff.

*

The brown face of Jesus,
captioned, *I drank from this cup
for your sake,* gazes at infinity
from a newspaper cut-out.

*

A photo of Idi Amin,
captioned in red letters, *The Butcher
of Uganda.*

*

A ravishing, blank-eyed white woman
in ripped denim shorts and see-through panties
lowers her body between the hips
of another woman.

*

In one hut, Blake's Nebuchadnezzar
crawls, half changed
to a lion, above the caption,
Consider this picture and repent,
or your punishment shall be like his.

*

A portrait of Mbuto,
captioned, *The most wicked*
man in Africa.

*

In one hut the haloed Christ,
his body healed, walks away
from the burial cave.

*

A white man buries his face
in a white girl's spread-eagled butt—
What do they do here? a village girl
carrying her baby asks her friend,
who shrugs as they walk away.

*

In one there is nothing
but a calendar.

*

In many there is nothing
but a gecko
holding its breath.

*

In most there are only spiders.

GREASE

When I felt my way out
of the windowless mud hut
on hands and knees to urinate
while the village slept,
I found, near the horizon, the brightest star,

but did not know which horizon,
or if it was the evening
or morning star. A thin bell tolled six times.
I searched for the outlines

of a mud wall where I had squatted in the dirt
with strangers around a kerosene lamp.
The shadows of hands,
mine huge and dark as theirs, had moved in silence
between caldron and mouths.
Grease dripped from fingers, lips, chins. Women and girls,
wives and second wives, ate by a lantern
in a far-off corner. Before earth and sun,
they say a solitary god
had made the Milky Way
by masturbating into the night.
Our grease smudges and teeth
flashed in dim lantern light.

Women had spent the day,
like every day, gathering dry cow dung
for cooking fires, scaring away children
and goats, spreading rice across the dirt to dry,
even as birds pecked at it,
then pounding it for hours
with pestle and mortar
until it was paste. Dinner

was when it got dark, we woke when it got light,
rested when it was hottest,
and slept at night. You shit
into a hole in the ground,
and when it's full
someone starts a new one.

Against the mud wall our giant hands
had closed around fistfuls of goat and rice paste,
then risen and opened
with quick, wet slapping sounds,
to monstrous shadows
of lips.

Arthur Rimbaud's Bad Leg

It did not come off in Abyssinia—
He made sure of that by paying
a fortune to be carried out—
twelve excruciating, brutal days
to the coast for all involved—
his litter, when necessary, placed on the ground,
so, scrabbling at the sand with both hands,
he could shift onto his side
to defecate.

> *A black, E white, I red, U green, O blue: vowels.*
> *One day I will tell of your latent births.*

The now-classic poems from his teens,
like any visionary work,
did not bring such a sum.
Ditto the obscene, adolescent,
homoerotic rhymes that followed:

> *A piece of cheese, a piece of shit...*

Not one centime came, nor was sought,
from the Paris bohemian literati
he lived off, tormented, and greeted
with such dinner tidings as,
I got fucked all night and can't
hold my shit—who just then
were publishing *Les Illuminations*.

The fortune Rimbaud paid
(worth a king's ransom or lifetimes
of back-breaking labor to most Africans,
though it was pocket change
from his Abyssinian profits)
did not come from the *Societe de Geographie,*
for whom he mapped and detailed the unknown
regions he journeyed through.

          I was indifferent to all crews,

proclaims his most famous poem, and so he was
to the laborers he supervised
in Cyprus—the malingering or simply slow
worker he killed with a dead-aimed
stone to the temple was his ticket
to Africa. His send-off,

years later, from Harar
to *terre inconnu* was carcasses
of cows, dogs, and goats
that ringed his home—angered by animals
urinating on pelts he left to dry,
he laced his perimeter
with strychnine.

Nor did Rimbaud wander through unknown lands
more heedless than the brains of children,
as prophesied in "The Drunken Boat."
He followed the trail
Menelik II had recently hacked and burned
across the Abyssinian interior—
young men slaughtered,
women and girls raped,

huts and crops torched,
infants, then children, followed by elders
starving to death
as Rimbaud found his way.

> *Lighter than a cork I danced on the waves*
> *that are called "eternal swells of victims."*

Rimbaud's king's ransom of a fortune
came, in fact, from the king.
Seeing what Menelik achieved
with stone-age weapons, realizing
the steady client he would be
for years to come, calculating
the premium the British and French ban
on musket and bullet exports
to the region would bring him,

Rimbaud earned his fortune
by way of the Remingtons,
Mausers, and Martins he sold to the king,
through which Rimbaud became the most prolific
arms dealer in the region,
and the king became Emperor
of Ethiopia, "Elect of God, Lion of Judah,
King of Kings," with enough firepower
left over to defeat the Italian army
years later.

It took forty minutes in Marseilles
to saw through Rimbaud's cancerous leg.

His mother had sent a letter from Roche
urging *Patience*. And his older sister—
forger of the sensitive,
bogus portrait of Rimbaud in white
robes, playing an Abyssinian harp
and gazing at the strings in reverie—
she began her lifelong quest to see
into how much more wealth she could turn
his legacy.

SAND

The hum of bees carrying
through walls of dry heat
was not bees but small boys
memorizing the Koran, reciting
half under their breath
the Arabic they know
only as the sound
of God.

Where two mud walls meet
I stepped into a gale
that rolled off the ocean
though there is no ocean
but desert, then there was no desert
but the sky turning
to orange-yellow drifts.

Each half *Mooo*
of a lost calf
was answered by the bleat of a goat
tied to a solitary tree.

When I left the village
to walk on the sea
of sand, I saw no one,
I heard nothing
but wind tearing itself
on a thorn bush. Beside a dune
a boy squatting to shit,
smiled, calling *Etranger. Light skinned guy*,
gesturing for me to come over.
You. Money. Money. Give me money.

In a trough I passed a pirogue
stranded until next summer
between two slow breakers of sand.

Before I could climb the second wave,
feet slipping and sinking,
five small boys blocked my way,
Demanding, *You! Money. Give me money.*

I turned—they blocked the way back.
Etranger. Give me a present.
In the village, in all the villages,
adults said, *Hit them. You have to hit them,*
and drove them off with a raised hand
and fierce monosyllables, the way children learned
to shoo away goats and donkeys.
Then the parents would ask for money.

I pointed to cow shit in the sand
near a boy's bare feet
and said to him, *There is your present.*
I pointed to a crock of donkey shit—
This is your money.
I was breathing sand.
I pointed to goat droppings—
These are your coins.
I drew my fist, seething, *Here is your gift.*
Hit them, adults would smile
Il faut frapper! Hit them, *etranger.* Hit them.

WAKING IN PEPERKOU, BENIN

In the village chief's hut
I woke alone
on the cement floor
to the sound of hooting.
It was the wind, I thought, an owl,
or doves cooing in the thatched eaves,
but there were no doves, just voices

of children, happy
as sunlight in fresh ponds
of morning air. A command
quieted them for moments
at a time. I slept once more,
among *Hoooo, hooo, owl, wind, owl.*

My first writing teacher
stood above my sleeping mat,
an exquisite, ankle-length *bou bou*
glistening against his now-black body.
Shards of sunlight pierced the thatched roof.
My face was buried in my arm.

What, he demanded in a dialect
two others translated,
*is your livelihood? Ten, now twenty years,
you have not succeeded.
Here, you fool these people.
They think you are important.
They think you are rich.
Their children crowd and stare as you scribble.*

My poems, I pleaded. *Listen. Just to <u>one</u>.*
He glowered down at my body. *These mean nothing.*
You waste your life. You must quit.
When I tried to reply he hit me
in the back of the head,
I flailed back at him
and woke with my right fist
pounding a basket of knotted ropes
in the chief's hut. I could hear
the hooting again, many children

making the sound of wind
whooshing through the diabolo's holes
when I twirled it and threw it into the sky.

Two silent faces gazed at me through the doorway—
I said, *The diabolo? Yes. I come,*
and there were cheers outside,
then chatter, like the dawn chirping
of many birds.

I showed the older children how to spin it,
and they showed the younger ones. A naked four-year-old
holding his penis stared in haunted-looking silence.
And toddlers too small to work the diabolo
stood in the dirt behind the others,
imitated the motion of twirling it,
then, jumping and laughing,
turned the motion of throwing the diabolo
into a dance, spreading their arms,
tossing into the air, over and over,
small sticks, handfuls of dirt and pebbles, and fragments
of a flattened soccer ball.

THE OPEN SEWERS OF MOPTI, MALI

Wide enough to kayak, useful—
until they overflow—for flood control, and deep
as a grave should be, locals call them *canals,*
as in the touts', *Welcome to Venice*
of West Africa. But late afternoon,
blocks from the madrassa, I heard a new inflection
of wind, then wind and surf
approach slowly and then break
into a hurricane of guttural shouts.

Sun flared for an instant
on the forehead of someone running.
A hail of rocks flew past him.
I saw his eyes flash white just before he stumbled.
People came running from sand alleyways.
The lead pursuer tackled him.
Someone pounded his face

again and again into the hard dirt street.
I don't know how else to put this.
Someone smashed a heavy stone
through his temple. I don't know
if his screams were words.
Older men with large knives
for slaughtering goats caught up, panting.

Boys caressing rocks
with frightening gentleness
circled slowly. There was a lot of yelling.
At the crowd's center a scrum of men
pressed waist-deep through a canal's sludge.

Crushed plastic bottles, a torn flip-flop,
a flattened soccer ball,
tatters of goat skin, and plastic bags

sat in the water's viscous stench—
so different from the flowing
robes girls and women
wash each day in the river,
so the men can glide over dirt streets
in billowing white gowns,
filled, like sails,
with sunlight.

Men and boys pushed in front of me.
I heard the loud thrashing of water.
The sewers are fed by shallow ditches
that start at a hole in the side
of each mud house. People milled around,

stared, chatted, and left the body
bleeding and half-drowned. Not the police,
not even the missing ghosts of his dead,
would touch him. Two boys,
side by side, tossed pebbles
at the bloodied scalp—
the sound muffled
like drizzle
on sand.

Thief, bad! people told me.
There was something about a sack of rice.
A small boy, then others, showed me their muscles.
America good. Bin Laden—
no good. Someone pointed to the sludge

that blackened his robe and smiled,
Thief. Voleur. Very bad. Je suis sale.
Cadeau. Cadeau. Donnez-moi un cadeau.
Give me a present
so I can make my grand boubou clean.

THE HELLO SONG

Antelope edge away slowly, then run:
Jaws stretched open, though still as corpses and breathless,
rows of teeth blazing with morning sun,
the *Hello* song of crocodiles is silence

and waiting. The turtle dove's is a constant
Tout a lou, tout a lou. An hour down a dirt road
toward Tanougou at noon, the *Hello* song
is bashful curtsies and smiles of underfed

girls and old women. They seek from me nothing
but a nod. From our open jeep, cheers
resolve into children's open-voweled chant,
Ca-deau, Ca-deau. From the weakest: just stares.

And danced, sung by toddlers in French they do not know—
a different, human, and true Song of Hello.

FUMES

1.

Since the colonizer's trucks
were bigger and more fearsome
than anything animal or human,
the faithful still form gods
from scavanged parts:

junked diesel tanks
are taken for torsos,
pistons for arms,
exhaust pipes, legs.
A tractor-trailer's coiled spring
is a god's tongue,
a carburetor his round head.

The god of evil's
heartless chest
is a steering wheel.
God of desire, god of procreation—
his thick erection
is a muffler.

2.

When the engine
of a bush taxi I rode in died,
we all got out to relieve themselves
while the driver found a straw
to suck gas and dirt
from the carburetor.
Then once again

we passed everything in sight,
the driver blasting his horn,
even at entire villages
of celebrants packing the half-paved road,
chanting, drumming, and dancing.

3.

Its cab gone, a tanker's
front end crushed
against the asphalt, gasoline
flowing like blood
of a dying animal,

people emerged joyfully
from the forest with water buckets,
to wait their turn
in the fumes rising on the gas-soaked road
for a few free liters,
to burn in their lamps.

4.

Day after day
the sand-filled fog
did not lift or breathe.
Not mist but Saharan dust
mixed with the leaded fumes
of moped-taxis that choke
the main road, searching
in swarms
for business.

5.

Dispensed, not from pumps
but in Bacardi, Seagram, Gordon's,
and anonymous other bottles, set out by size
on make-shift tables—
the gasoline's golden tint,
the heat, and thirst tricked me
to crave it
as cider.

6.

Aziz, in Paradise
Bar and Restaurant,
introduced himself with, *You drink all night —
On my wallet.* His flowing hand gesture
shoos from the table

the cute girl whose place he gave me—
Just my friend, he says;
later, *My little sister,*
later still, *A whore.*
I am Moslem but not strict.
He is half drunk.
His work is to buy cars
where they are cheap
and sell them where they are not.
The flash cube explodes
in the mirror behind the liquor bottles
in the photo he sent of me and him.
He has wives in two countries,
children in four.
He raises his glass to toast me—
Bush. Strong. Bush promised war.
And there is war.

THE FRENCH MILITARY CEMETERY OF OUIDAH, BENIN

Each bronze plaque
  is set in a bed
    of light—

brown gravel.
  Each lies in a frame
    of white-

washed concrete
  Two-meter high walls
    guard the graves

from view.
  Their whitewash,
    on which I steadied

the camera
  to take the photo
    from which I write,

is clean
  as the sun.
    At the head

of each grave
  a bronze cross
    rises

five inches
  in stunted
    resurrection.

On a dais
    of gravel
        set off by a hedgerow,

a frigate captain's
    pyramid-shaped tomb
        embossed with an anchor

stands over
    the meticulously spaced
        rows and files.

The sand
    is swept
        from the graves.

The leaves
    are swept
        to a corner.

Six dead even
    rows of eight
        graves each

are set in the colonialist's
    symmetry and rage
        for order,

so different
    from the African
        graveyards

in the forests,
    the overgrown
        raw cement,

some graves
      without stones,
            some stones

without names,
      some tombs broken
            and vacant—

so different
      from Ouidah's largest graveyard,
            the sea,

on which most slaves
      sold here
            died in transport,

or in the holds
      of ships
            awaiting transport,

the white of the waves,
      their markers
            and epitaphs,

the white of the waves
      likewise as clean
            as the sun.

IV

WANT

When the scars
that were hints
of a road turned
to nothing,
I found the dark insect
that is the plane's shadow.

Just past dawn,
through the sudden blaze of Saharan light,
I followed the channel
of a river
of wind.

A whaleback
sixty miles long
broke into white-cap waves
of sand.

A wind-wrecked ridge
turned to spires
of a ruined city.

This fragment
of a tomb
for your camera,
someone had offered.

This club,
to batter the sun-
baked ground, to plant
a handful of peanuts—this club
for your passport.

Since the voices
in the desert
are the last
to be trusted,
I listened harder.

When the sky turned to sand
I heard again the dull rage
of the harmattan
rising and falling
in the nettles.

What I took
for dwellings turned to shadows
of rock.

    Your money for my friendship.
    Your food for my hunger.

Since the visions
in the desert
are the last to be trusted,
I looked harder.

I found, for a moment,
The body of the snake
that is the Niger River.
When the sand between the ridges
turned to inlets, I hunted for the secret spires
of the sea.

Beggars of Cotonou, Benin

One old man slipped the five stumps
of his leprosy-eaten fingers
through my open window
in a bush-taxi
and held them there.

A fifteen-year-old girl,
flirtatious and beautiful,
draped her fingers around the bulge
of my wallet and smiled like a would-be lover,
What's that?

Hunched, shriveled, and solitary,
pressing three fingers against her thumb,
a woman gestured over and over
to her open mouth,
and glared at me.

Three boys, when told, *It is not good
to ask a visitor for money,*
said, *What then do you ask?,*
became my friends,
showed me the magazine cut-outs
of white models and singers
on their hut walls,
and asked for nothing.

One man pointed
the short stump
of his right shoulder at me,
and as he tried to wave, *Hello,*
it just twitched
back and forth.

One just pointed
to his pupil-less, yellowed eyes.

After receiving twelve cents
in what was left
of both hands, one waited twenty minutes
for me to return with my camera
so he could keep his promise
to pose for me.

In high, vinyl boots despite the heat,
a short, clingy shirt, and stretch jeans,
one woman sat down at my table,
saying, *Buy me a drink.*
Buy me a meal. Like yours.

Two women hurried
across a three-block expanse of dirt
to jab open palms again and again
at the air beneath my chin.

Chanting fiercely,
naked above the waist,
and wielding a long knife,
one man approached me,
pressed the blade
into his cheek, his throat,
wrapped the skin
of his eyelid around the point,
then removed a long-haired wig,
turned it upside-down, so it took the shape of a bowl,
smiled and thanked me
for a few coins.

One girl said, *Because I'm cute,*
smart, poor, and you are rich.

Three boys said, *Because we are your friends.*

One boy said, *Because*
I gave you directions.

Most said nothing.

One just said, *Because.*

Cafe Baobab

Soldiers come. At night. Kill my family.
I run. They shoot—my mother, my father—
Please. Say your name. Then we go—embassy.

Here—no work. They stamp my visa, *Refugee*.
I run. The forest. They kill my neighbors.
Night. Then—*my* house. They kill my family.

They take from my house. What they can carry.
I try for work. Taxi-man. Bar man. Seller.
Say again your name. We go? U.S. embassy.

You tell them—*I am your friend. You help me.*
You give job. They kill my small sister.
Soldiers. Night. Tell them, *They kill my family.*

Not possible for me in your country?
Europe—we try. You tell them, *Congo. War.*
We go. You and me. You talk. To French embassy.

I not ask for *cadeau*. Ask no one money.
You tell my story. You. A writer!
Night, soldiers come they kill my family.
You come. We try. Maybe Canada embassy.

DRUMMING

1.

Walking the slave route
from the Point of No Return
to the ocean,
I could not tell if the cries I heard
were men imitating animals
or animals mimicking men.
Something began hooting.
I did not know
if the thumping that came from the forest
off and on all afternoon
was ceremony or labor,
drum or hammer.

2.

The drumming
in villages, morning to dusk,
is women and children,
pestle and mortar
pounding millet into paste.

3.

With neither plow nor harrow,
the hollow *Thud, thud, thud*
just beyond the village
is men with axes and clubs
beating open
the dry ground.

4.

Where three dirt paths meet,
their naked backs caked with sand,
forty women dance half naked
around a spreading mango tree—
the big wife, as men put it,
slimmer second and third wives,

and teen-age girls, naked breasts
glistening with sweat and moonlight,
bald women without teeth,

and pubescent girls—
all lowering their bodies
toward the sandy earth,
elbows, like wings,
beating the air
into the dirt, and singing
thanks and prayers for harvests
past, passing, and to come.

GIRLS AND WOMEN OF BENIN

As I crouch before an altar at Temple Yoho,
an old woman appears, offering me
a bowl of rice and a cup of sacred water.

On Natitingou's dirt main street
girls and old women lower their eyes,
smile bashfully, and curtsy before me.

I try to return an old woman's bow
but cannot match its grace
and sweetness.

The small girl in Peperkou
on whose head the diabolo crashes
after I throw it high as I can
stifles cries and tears
when I touch her scalp
and say *I am sorry*
in French she does not know.

A woman squats on the sidewalk
in Porto Novo, holds up the hem
of her long skirt
and urinates prodigiously.

One woman vendor wears an Osama bin Laden
T-shirt, but her son says
she does not know who he is.

A ten-year-old girl slams her forehead
over and over into the asphalt road
leading out of Parakou,
screaming, *I sold fruit all day*
then someone stole the money.

Five girls in their teens wait day and night
between a speed bump and a check point
on the road to Cotonou,
so they can race after bush taxis
to sell small plastic bags
of water.

One woman makes loud animal cries
into the forest, and listens
for her companions,
to gauge how far they are
from her.

A young woman stands half naked, alone
in the bush, finds my eyes, and smiles shyly
into them as the train I ride
gathers speed.

At a market outside Djougou,
three girls from a tribal group I have never seen—
sun-white cowrie shells
sewn into pure black foreheads at their eyebrows —
stare at me in the silence and wonder
through which I keep stealing glances
at them.

Where houses are built
as small mud fortresses,
a village woman with no front teeth
takes my hand in her scaly palm,
begins to sing, then dance,
pushing her chest against mine,
then her groin, pressing and laughing
harder and harder.

COTONOU AT NIGHT

No stars
      since the night sky
         is a cloud
            of sand,

no streetlights,
      but on makeshift tables
         small fires
            in braziers

form constellations
      of families
         cooking dinner
            and chatting quietly,

squatting on dirt sidewalks
      beside dirt streets.
         Their haloes
            of dust

are simply dust
      and heat.
         Children play quietly
            until they go to sleep

on dusty mats.
      Their mothers' chat
         and clean pots
            until they lie down

beside them.
    A big picnic,
        no school
            the next day,

was my impression
    the first night
        I wandered
            through Cotonou.

Through the grit-filled darkness
    people greet
        my light face
            with, *Bon soir, Monsieur,*

and ask
    for nothing
        but to see
            if I am lost.

Two years ago here
    foreigners, mainly,
        were chased, butchered,
            or lit on fire

by mobs
    set off
        again and again
            by lone screams,

He stole my penis!
    since the art of voodoo
        makes this possible
            with a handshake

or incantation.
      Good Samaritans
            fueled by the goodness
                of the righteous

is how they must have
      seen themselves
            giving chase
                each time
to the culprit
      and to those
            who tried to offer
                sanctuary—

as they stripped
      the guilty naked,
            splashed the kerosene,
                struck the matches,

or wielded the axes.
      Now the bodies
            I see are large families,
                sleeping

in tight clusters.
      I find my way
            through the night
                to the jury-rigged street stand

of the lady
      who sells me water.
            I watch her small girl
                gently wake her

so she can greet me,
       delicately wipe the night's grit
           from the plastic bottle,
                wish me and my family well,

then offer it to me
      shyly
            at the best price I know
            in Cotonou.

V

SOUNDING THE NAMES

Since the language has no word list,
the village no school or history
of strangers, since the river
is the only real way there, the half-visible

sandy track beside it
in the dry season the only alternate...
Since the translated, phonetic
phrases I'd gotten were the wrong dialect,

when I arrived they sounded out the names
for what they could point to:
goats and chickens wandering around,
a bucket of dying fish, the pirogue

they caught them from. The word
in the desert for *water*
was *manna*, though I could not point
to *desert* since it was everywhere.

Sun and *moon*,
and the dry cow dung
gathered each morning
for cooking fuel were easy.

So were *hand, teeth, lips,*
tongue, and when Pama got to *breast*
she pushed aside her gown,
pinched her nipple, and waited
for me to repeat. *Chie.*

Chie—making my "*Ch*"
more guttural. *Chie, Chie*
to fix my inflection.

When I pointed to the palm tree
high above the mud huts,
I do not know if the word
they gave me was for *tree*, the clutch

of coconuts in its high groin,
or *green, or wind, wind*
ripping through fronds,
or *wind-blown sand.*

A boy pulled his pants down
pointed to his penis,
and said the word slowly,
making sure I wrote it—

Cock? Dick? Penis?
Did they tell me *floor*
or *hard mud? Sky* or *blue?*
Money was clear or was it

Give me money
when the hand waving *Hello*
deftly flipped to a jaunty
right angle with my chin.

Pama taught me
three types of bowls,
two types of fish traps,
the word for grinding millet

with pestle and mortar, words
for *bracelet* and *ring*.
Fuck was clear enough—
two fingers shoved

into the tight circle
of forefinger and thumb.
Her pantomime was clear
as a paragraph—pointing from her body to mine,

hands slowly swelling
her dress into a pregnant oval
at her stomach.
A long, rising vowel—

not a word
or else pure onomatopoeia—
a beatific smile
showing the missing

and discolored teeth, a hand
gesturing somewhere
beyond the river and desert,
her smile held so long

it froze from summer dream
to a half-toothless woman's
hopeless plea.
Two small boys took turns

mimicking seductive dances
until she shooed them off
with quick, guttural syllables.
I had no way to ask the words

for *Why?* and *How?*
or to say, *I am leaving soon,*
so she wouldn't spend
half the next day fixing my dinner—none

for *happy* or *sad, yesterday*
or *tomorrow*, none for the sea
between *talk* and *fuck,*
nor the desert between *gone* and *here.*

WIND

In the morning, subdued—
a drunk who gets loud
as the day wears on.

Three afternoon musket shots
echoing off the wind-
swept cliffs mean a dead man's spirit,
overstaying its time in the village,
is driven to the bush
to start the awful journey
to paradise.

Late afternoon breezes shifting directions,
carrying the voices of children
from the four corners of the village,
mean all is well.

The harmattan at night
tearing through the forest—
girls and women
keep to their huts,
where the half-visible
spirits of the bush
cannot make them pregnant
with their monstrous progeny.

Leaves rustling
at the edges of the village—
the year's dead
are restless again.
They pace the air, plead

to rejoin their families
in the flesh
of the next-born infant,
gusting, subsiding, and murmuring prayers
for breath.

FINDING AMADOU'S GRANDFATHER IN NORTHERN TOGO

1.

He is dozing
    behind the trunk
        of a baobab tree

when I come to him.
    He stirs then sits.
        His eyes are like my grandfather's

on days he tells me
    he can remember
        nothing.

2.

Is Amadau, he asks,
    the city,
        village,

or European name
    of my grandson?
        First name or second?

Is he now a man?
    A boy?
        Is his family well?

3.

Cracks traverse his adobe hut.
      His remaining children here
            are deformed and dying

millet plants
      in the dirt patch
            beyond the baobab tree.

Over the baying
      of a mother goat
            sharing the shade with us

I nod
      at words I pick out
            in his pidgin French.

Somewhere in a field
      of tall dead grass
            his bad leg,

which went septic
      and was sawed off
            in the 1950s,

has grown
      into a thorn tree—
            arthritic

branches, twisted
      against the harmattan,
            scraping the wind.

The village *patrons,*
    his life-long bosses,
        are two brothers,

dry earth
    and *dry wind.*
        His once-supple lover,

the rain,
    is a whore
        who brought malaria

years ago
    then left
        without a word.

His last
    surviving wife
        is *drought.*

He says I can photograph him,
    but not the two mud gods
        that watch his home,

not the gully beside them
    that channels sacrificial blood
        to his millet patch.

He squints to recall
    There is a mango tree
        in Amadou's courtyard?

But all courtyards
    in this country
        have mango trees.

He has twenty or thirty
       grandchildren still living,
          he tells me.

4.

He asks
       something
          I do not follow,

about tea.
       He rises slowly,
          like a tide,

against his long straight stave,
       his one leg
          thick with sores

and swollen.
       He says, *Monsieur. S'il vous plait.*
          You come? Home? With me?

THE PRESIDENT'S MAUSOLEUM
OUTSIDE NATITINGOU, BENIN

Because the first emperor did not die
but achieved immortality as a tree,
and when the tree was cut
its stump grew taller than before...

Because the king
resisting the French
escaped, for a time,
by changing himself to a shark,

and in nearby Togo
the President for Life
is everywhere—his photo
behind hotel desks,

on dirt-stained billboards,
the T-shirts, now torn,
distributed each "election" time for free,
emblazoned, *Peace, Security, Progress.*

Even in suit and tie,
he appears as a goon—
the unblinking stare
of a snake, aware how motionlessly

it must wait. So here, the mausoleum
of the once-absolute
ruler, three high stories of blinding white marble,
is the tallest, most solid

structure in the province—
cathedral windows in a region
where glass is rare. The long entranceway
up the hill it sits on

is dirt and stubble. At its foot
a locked bicycle chain holds shut
the aristocratically grand gate.
It rusts and flakes paint in a field of weeds

along the road to Natitingou—blocking nothing
since no fence or wall remains.
Nothing and no one
care to go around it

but four stray goats
up to their haunches
in the sloping lawn
of thistles.   Atop the mausoleum

rise the white false teeth
of faux battlements—
somebody's idea
of a chateau.

The surrounding brambles
and stubble are charred
here and there as if someone
kept trying and failing

to burn it. The language
of the architecture and fresh white paint
translates to, *Keep Out,*
that of the rest to, *Why bother?*

ANDREW KAUFMAN grew up near NYC, graduated from Oberlin College, earned his MFA in poetry writing from Brooklyn College, and his MA and Ph.D. in English Literature from the University of Toronto. His *Cinnamon Bay Sonnets* won the Center for Book Arts chapbook competition, and was followed by *Earth's Ends*, winner of the Pearl Poetry Award. He is the recipient of an NEA award and two Pushcart poetry nominations, and his poems have appeared in numerous journals. He has also published critical work on William Blake, and written for *New York Newsday* and *The Detroit News*. He lives in New York City and currently teaches literature at SUNY Purchase.

S P U Y T E N   D U Y V I L

Meeting Eyes Bindery
Triton
Lithic Scatter

www.ingramcontent.com/pod-product-compliance
Lightning Source LLC
Chambersburg PA
CBHW020921090426
42736CB00008B/733